Us

Children's Readers in the Classroom

A Handbook for Teachers

Michael Philips and Jenny van der Walt

Heinemann Educational Publishers
Halley Court, Jordan Hill, Oxford OX2 8EJ
A Division of Reed Educational & Professional Publishing Ltd

Heinemann Educational Books (Nigeria) Ltd
PMB 5205, Ibadan
Heinemann Educational Botswana (Publishers) (Pty) Ltd
PO Box 10103, Village Post Office, Gaborone, Botswana

FLORENCE PRAGUE MADRID ATHENS
MELBOURNE AUCKLAND TOKYO SINGAPORE KUALA LUMPUR
PORTSMOUTH NH (USA) MEXICO CITY CHICAGO
SAO PAULO JOHANNESBURG KAMPALA NAIROBI

First published by Heinemann Educational Publishers in 1997

British Library Cataloguing in Publication Data
A catalogue record for this book is available from the British Library

Cover and text designed by Susan Clarke
Illustrated by Helen Averley

ISBN 0 435 890 980

Printed and bound in Great Britain by
Biddles Ltd, Guildford and King's Lynn

Acknowledgements
The authors and publishers would like to thank the following for their permission to use copyright material:

Pages 34–5, Lionel Murcott for his poem 'The Winterman', © Lionel Murcott 1988, first published in its original form in *My Drum* by Abecedarius Books and The Hippogriff Press, South Africa, and also published in its present form in a limited edition of Lionel Murcott's poems: *The Winterman and Other Poems for Children* by Piglet Press, Johannesburg (1995); page 43, Maskew Miller Longman, Cape Town, for the shape poem, taken from page 149 of *English Comprehensive Practice 5* (5th edition, 1993) by Goodacre and Rumboll; pages 75–6, Faber & Faber Ltd for 'Funeral Blues' from 'Twelve Songs' in *Collected Poems* by W.H. Auden.

The publishers have made every effort to trace copyright holders, but if anyone has been inadvertently overlooked or incorrectly cited, please let the publishers know and they will make the necessary changes at the first opportunity.

97 98 99 10 9 8 7 6 5 4 3 2 1

Contents

To the teacher

The Junior African Writers Series – JAWS – has been very well received in African classrooms. We have been using readers in the series for a number of years. We have found them useful in developing our pupils' fluency in English and our pupils have enjoyed reading the stories from cover to cover.

As teachers, we all experience difficulties. Some of the problems which you may share are:

- English is not your own home language, but you have to teach it.
- Pupils themselves have different home languages – few have English as a mother tongue.
- Pupils have little opportunity to practise speaking and writing in English.
- There is a lack of resource material.

When we found ourselves facing some of these problems, we worked together to find solutions. We decided to use the JAWS readers because they reflect African life. Stories set in different countries allowed our pupils to share in the culture and experiences of people throughout Africa. Also, JAWS readers are graded, in five levels of complexity, making them suitable for pupils with different abilities and language competencies.

Our main aim was to use JAWS readers to develop language activities which would encourage confidence and ability in English through reading, writing and speaking. In addition, we have found the readers very useful across the curriculum; they stimulate study in other areas such as maths, history and art.

All the activities in this book have been tried and tested with pupils in the classroom. The ideas are practical and are relevant to the pupils' real-life experiences.

All teachers can use JAWS as a basis for original and creative lessons. We hope that you will enjoy using and adapting the activities in your own classrooms, whether you are new to teaching or more experienced. We have had great success with JAWS. By sharing our ideas, we hope that other teachers and pupils can also experience such success.

Michael Philips
Jenny van der Walt

How this book works

We have divided the book into four sections, as follows:

1 Choosing JAWS titles (Chapter 1)
We suggest some things to bear in mind before making your choice, and give advice on ordering the titles you do choose. We also give some practical ideas on using the books in the classroom: how to organise their collection and distribution.

2 Skills-based teaching (Chapter 2)
This is our tried and tested approach to teaching, and we describe the various elements of the four main skills. We set out a 'skills grid' on pages 6–7 to identify those skills. Each one is matched to activities in one of the five JAWS levels.

3 Activities: Levels 1 to 5 (Chapters 3–7)
This is the main part of the book, where we describe activities that will help pupils attain those skills. This section is divided into five chapters: each chapter deals with one of the JAWS levels, in sequence. For each level, we suggest certain activities related to the various skills. We have used two different JAWS titles for each of Levels 1 to 3, and one for the more advanced Levels 4 and 5. These particular titles happen to have worked well for us; in case they are not available to you, we give a brief synopsis of the story to set the activities in context. However, we emphasise that you should feel free to choose any JAWS readers you like and adapt our ideas to suit your own situation. (Indeed, should you not have access to JAWS books, the material here can be adapted perfectly well to other series of readers.)

To show how our ideas have worked in practice, we reproduce our study plan for using one of the Level 3 JAWS readers as a theme in English.

At the end of each chapter, after the skills-related activities, there is a section on 'Integration'. Here, we give suggestions on how to use the readers in a wider context, for other subject areas in the curriculum. For example, on page 25, we show how a Level 1 reader, *The Frightened Thief*, can provide activities related to maths, health and life skills.

4 Record-keeping and assessment (Chapter 8)

Effective teaching needs the back-up of good organisation. Here, we give ideas for assessing pupils' progress and keeping records, again based on our own practical experience.

1 Choosing JAWS titles

The themes in the JAWS series are rich and varied, appealing to both boys and girls of different ages. There are mysteries, romances, comedies, crime stories, stories about the environment, fantasies, action adventures and the more traditional kinds of story. JAWS titles and their themes are listed on page 87.

The stories are set in different African countries, so the series has a pan-African appeal. You can choose local stories, or stories set in other countries.

The JAWS readers are graded into five levels of difficulty. The levels differ in length, print size and language complexity. The lowest levels, 1 and 2, have a continuous narrative (i.e. not divided into chapters). The higher levels are divided into chapters. All the stories are illustrated in a lively and realistic style, helping children (especially the younger ones) understand the text. Levels 1 and 2 have illustrations on every page, while the others have 10 to 12 full-page illustrations with captions.

Each JAWS reader has a short section at the back of the book, to test pupils' responses to the story. Levels 1 to 4 have comprehension questions on the text, plus a number of activities suggesting further development of ideas. In addition, they have a glossary of the more difficult words, while some books also have a glossary of African words used in the text. Level 5 titles, being rather more demanding and thought-provoking, just have a section suggesting related topics for discussion.

On page 85, we suggest compiling and storing answers to those questions in the readers. How you use the questions in class – and the activities, glossary and discussion topics too – in relation to the activities suggested in this book, is up to you. You may find that you can integrate them to a greater or lesser extent.

The JAWS books you select will depend on your pupils' interests, needs, and reading and language ability. It is useful to have a range of levels in the classroom so that pupils can begin at a level they feel comfortable with and progress upwards. However, you might find that pupils can read at a high level, but that they choose books from lower levels because they like the themes. This is quite normal. You might also find that some pupils like to read the same story over and over. This is also normal and, although you should encourage them to branch out, you should not stop pupils from reading simply for enjoyment.

To help you make a choice from the JAWS series, Heinemann publishes a catalogue every year, which you can obtain by writing to the address at the back of this book.

Organising JAWS as classroom readers

You need to develop a system that is practical and effective for you. Teachers work in different conditions: what works in one school may not work in another. The important thing is to develop some system of organising the books and keeping control of who uses them. Pupils must be taught to handle books – such a valuable investment – with respect.

Share ideas with colleagues and other teachers in your district; perhaps they in turn have ideas that you can use. Meanwhile, here are some of the methods which we have tried and which have worked well for us.

Issuing books

- Number the books, and write out a checklist of the numbers and the relevant titles.
- Keep a record of who takes each book – the form shown gives an idea of how to keep track. (NB: a circled number shows that the book has been returned.)

Pupil's name	Books taken out
Xola Mati	② 12
Ntusi Moloi	④ ③ 2
etc.	

- If there are not enough copies for everyone, get pupils to share copies.
- Where pupils need to share books, both or all are responsible for the book.
- Ideally, cover books with plastic before issuing them. This is a bit expensive, but it does preserve the books.

Storing the books

- Cardboard boxes make good book containers. The boxes can be placed on their sides in the classroom and used as bookcases (see illustration below). They can also be picked up and stored safely if necessary.
- Show your pupils how to store the books with their spines outwards, so the titles (on the thicker books) are visible.
- The boxes can be painted or covered with pictures to make them look attractive.
- To stop the books getting dirty, tell your pupils to make sure their hands are clean before using them. The pupils should also be reminded not to eat anything while reading the books.

2 Skills-based teaching

One traditional way of teaching is called the 'chalk and talk' approach. Teachers talk at their pupils and hope they are listening. The pupils are passive, not actively involved. The focus is always on the content.

In contrast, the way of teaching that we follow, the skills-based approach, demands the active participation of the pupils. In a lesson they are busy, working together. They share their knowledge; they speak, explore and learn from each other. The focus in such an approach is on the useful skills which the pupils learn. These skills help them discover and learn content by themselves.

Skills are essential as they are the key to understanding. Rote-learning often leads to confusion, and pupils very often forget what they have learned. Skills-based teaching gives them the tools to find knowledge as and when they need to. This handbook encourages the development of this approach to teaching and learning, which may be summarised as follows:

- Pupils are responsible for their own learning.
- Pupils are encouraged to become actively involved in the process of developing skills.
- Pupils are given the opportunity to think, argue, discuss, solve problems, explore and discover knowledge.

Skills checklist

The grid on pages 6–7 summarises the skills covered in this book. There are four main groups: oral skills, reading skills, language skills and writing skills. These groups are identified in the first column on the left. Each group is broken down into different elements, under each level of JAWS reader (see Levels 1–5 across the top of the grid). If you move down the grid, you will see that all four skill groups are covered in each JAWS level.

Oral skills

Naturally, these involve the spoken word. To encourage fluency and confidence, we suggest activities including reading aloud, discussion, drama, speech-making, interviews and a variety of role-paying situations. Some of them may require written preparation too.

Reading skills

These go beyond simply deciphering words. The activities we suggest encourage thorough comprehension of language, its structure and style, and appreciation of character and plot in a story.

Language skills

The study of formal language – grammar, punctuation and meanings of words – may be rather off-putting to pupils if taught on its own. We find that nouns, adjectives, verbs and so on can be made much more meaningful if they can be seen to work directly in a story. Accordingly, the activities we suggest are geared to this.

Writing skills

Whether involving prose or poetry, these activities encourage imagination as well as the practical, manual exercise of writing.

The grid on the next spread shows only the skills that we have covered here. You may well think of others.

	JAWS Level 1	JAWS Level 2
Oral skills	Questioning and discussion (10) Dialogue (11) Interviews (12) Drama (12)	Questioning (31) Group discussions (32) Giving a speech (33) Role play (33) Poetry reading (34)
Reading skills	Predicting outcomes (13) Comprehension (13) Sequencing the story (15)	Multiple-choice comprehension (35) Distinguishing cause and effect (37) Analysing setting and plot (37) Collecting related newspaper articles (38) Identifying the author's intentions (38)
Language skills	Punctuation (17) Verbs (18) Tenses (18) Proper nouns (19) Dictionary work (19)	Direct speech (39) Contractions (40) Adjectives (40) Figurative language – similes (41)
Writing skills	Writing a note (20) Filling in a form (21) Writing a rhyming chant (22) Writing a summary (23) Producing a comic strip (24) Paragraph writing (25)	Newspaper reports (41) Praise poetry (42) Shape poems (43) 'Spelling' poems (43) Slogans (44) Memorandums (44)

JAWS Level 3	JAWS Level 4	JAWS Level 5
Analysing the book's cover (48) Memorising details (49) Introductions (50) Discussions and debates (51)	Addressing people (63)	Poetry (75) Expressing condolences (76) Themes and issues (77) Character judgements (77)
How punctuation works (51)	Reading for the main idea (64) Summarising content (65) Reading for information (66)	Character boxes (77) Inferential reading (78)
Vocabulary (52) Similes (53)	Abbreviations (67) Adjectives and adverbs (68) Pronouns (69) Prepositions (70)	Emotive language (78) Indirect speech (79) Plurals (79)
Invitations (53) Spray diagrams (55) Using the senses (55) Advertisements (56) Crossword puzzle (59) Questionnaire (60)	Concise language (71) Writing a letter (71) Writing a diary (72)	Paragraph writing (79) Letter of condolence (80) Writing a report (81) Writing a script (81)

3 Activities for Level 1

At this level, the pupils are probably beginning to develop confidence in using English. They will need a lot of support and encouragement from you. They will also need to work through carefully structured and manageable activities such as those in this section.

Activities are completed as the pupils read through the book.

We have selected two titles: *The Frightened Thief* by Amu Djoleto and *Weird Wambo* by Gaele Mogwe. However, we emphasise that you should feel free to try the activities with any Level 1 title.

SYNOPSES

The Frightened Thief is set in Ghana. Amanor is twelve and lives with his mother, who runs a kiosk. His father runs a shop and lives apart from them. Amanor is given pocket money by both his mother and his father. He does not have many friends at school; his best friends are two girls. Amanor is bullied by two bigger boys, who demand money from him. Afraid, Amanor breaks into the cupboard in his classroom and steals money; he is caught red-handed by Mr Kotei, who tells Amanor's teacher, Miss Peku. Amanor then runs away, and ends up selling sweets on the street. He is knocked down in the road and wakes up in hospital, to realise that he has done wrong and to be reconciled with family and school.

Weird Wambo is set in Botswana. Wambo is a young woman who lives alone in a baobab tree. The villagers shun or torment her because she is 'weird' (make sure your pupils understand the meaning of this word). One day some local children are playing in the bush and a little boy falls down a hole. Diane, the oldest child, goes to Wambo for help. Diane is surprised to find that Wambo's home is clean, neat and nicely furnished. Wambo helps to pull up the little boy and carries him back to her home; the other children come too, and Wambo looks after them all. She tells Diane her story: she had refused all suitors for her hand, not feeling ready for marriage. The people in her village began to think she was odd, so she ran away to live alone. The children are very impressed with her beauty and kindness.

Using both readers, we have focused on the following skills and suggested relevant activities.

Oral skills

- questioning and discussion
- dialogue
- interviews
- drama

Reading skills

- predicting outcomes
- comprehension
- sequencing the story

Language skills

- punctuation
- verbs
- tenses
- proper nouns
- dictionary work

Writing skills

- writing a note
- filling in a form

- writing a rhyming chant
- writing a summary
- producing a comic strip
- paragraph writing

Oral skills

It is important to allow pupils to practise speaking the language. As they develop their oral skills, they are able to express themselves confidently and to form and voice their own opinions. The following activities can help in this process, and give the pupils the chance to explore the issues raised in the stories. Some of the activities also involve writing skills (when written words are to be read aloud), but the focus here is on oral expression.

Questioning and discussion

Children need to learn that there are different 'question' words, mainly:

- which?
- what?
- why?
- where?
- when?
- who?
- how?

They also need to learn that some questions may need only 'yes' or 'no' answers, while others are more open-ended.

Referring to *The Frightened Thief*, you might like to encourage a class discussion around pocket money. (You might need to start by asking the pupils if they know what it is and why it is given. This would help children in low-income families, who may not be familiar with the concept, to understand its relevance in the story.)

You could ask your pupils questions like:

- **Why do you think the parents in the story gave Amanor pocket money?**
- **What would you do with pocket money?**
- **Should children work to earn pocket money?**

However, you must remember that there are no absolutely correct answers in these discussions. You should encourage your pupils to answer honestly and creatively.

Dialogue

Reading and writing are skills that go together. It is often useful to develop both at the same time. In this activity the pupils learn how to make up a dialogue (conversation).

The pupils should work in pairs. As an introduction, they should take turns to ask each other questions and talk about their families. Working in pairs allows the pupils to develop conversation skills.

After this oral activity, the teacher can show the pupils how to write a dialogue (see also page 17 for some work on punctuation), as in the example below.

> **Sipho: What are you going to do during the school holidays?**
>
> **Maria: I am staying at home. We cannot afford a holiday this year.**
>
> **Sipho: I am going to my aunt and uncle in Dar es Salaam.**
>
> **Maria: You visited them last year as well, didn't you?**
>
> **Sipho: Yes, I did. They have no children of their own, so they like to see me.**

Once the pupils know how to construct a dialogue, you can turn back to *The Frightened Thief* and ask them to make up a dialogue between a school bully and another pupil. Once again they can work in pairs. Having written down their dialogue, they could then read it out for the other pupils.

Interviews

This is a similar activity to the previous one. You could show your pupils how an interview (whether for radio, television or a newspaper article) is structured, using an example like the one below. You could write it on the chalk board or interview one of your pupils.

Interviewer: When are you touring Africa?

Ismaël Lo: I'll be in Senegal and Gambia in September.

Interviewer: And after that?

Ismaël Lo: I hope to return to Paris to record a new song.

Make sure the pupils understand how an interview is structured. Then, using *Weird Wambo* for reference, divide the class into pairs. One pupil is the interviewer, while the other is Weird Wambo herself. Give them time to think up their questions and answers, and to practise the interview (possibly also writing it down). After this they can perform for the class.

Drama

Divide *Weird Wambo* into separate parts. Divide the class into groups and give each group a different part of the story. The groups re-read their parts and then act them out for the rest of the class.

Reading skills

We focus here on three important areas: predicting outcomes, comprehension and (an associated skill) sequencing the story.

Predicting outcomes

As you read the story aloud to your pupils, you can stop here and there and ask them what they think will happen next. This is called predicting. Predicting allows you to see whether pupils are understanding the story. It also gives pupils the chance to use their imaginations and express their own ideas. Predicting outcomes also helps pupils to develop their concept of story.

For example, in *The Frightened Thief* Amanor is caught stealing from Miss Peku's cupboard by Mr Kotei. At this stage, you could stop the reading and ask the pupils what they think will happen next. You should give them a few minutes to think alone before allowing discussion. Discussion could involve the whole class, or pupils could talk to each other in small groups.

Comprehension

Comprehension exercises should contain a range of different types of question. A comprehension exercise which requires pupils only to find rote answers in the text does not really test whether they understand or not.

Here is an example of a comprehension exercise on *The Frightened Thief*, containing different types of question. (Note: these questions touch on details far beyond the brief synopsis given on page 8; if you do not have access to this particular reader, rest assured that the relevant information is there in the story. These questions simply suggest an appropriate range.)

1 Where does Amanor live?

2 What is Amanor's favourite food?

3 Why does Amanor receive so much pocket money?

4 Who are Amanor's best friends?

5 How old is Amanor?

6 What is the name of the school in the story?

7 Name the two school bullies.

8 What do the bullies want from Amanor?

9 Who sees Amanor at Miss Peku's cupboard?

10 What does Miss Peku keep in the cupboard?

11 Why does Amanor's mother come to school the next day?

12 Where does Damey see Amanor?

13 How is Amanor knocked down?

14 What is a kiosk?

15 Why do you think Amanor lies and steals?

16 How do you feel when someone teases you?

17 When Miss Peku asks Amanor why he has broken into the cupboard, he looks at the ground. Why do you think he looks at the ground?

18 How do you think Amanor feels when Miss Peku tells him that his parents will have to see the headmistress?

19 What lesson do you think Amanor learns from his experience?

The first 13 questions require basic comprehension only. These questions assess whether your pupils have followed the story. You should encourage them to refer to the story to find the answers. Referring to the story encourages skimming and reading for information – skills we need in real life to read timetables, phone books, information signs and so on.

Question 14 is the type of question that encourages pupils to use the glossary at the back of the book, or a dictionary. You could include synonyms and opposites in this kind of question as well.

The last five questions require the pupils to express their own ideas and opinions. The pupils learn to understand that there are different answers to questions. Through questions like this, the pupils learn to make decisions and judgements based on their own experiences. This can make the study of literature come to life for them.

Sequencing the story

Sequencing the story is an important skill. It requires the pupils to place sentences or events in the correct order. Sequencing enables you to check that the pupils have followed the plot of the story and that they can understand what they are reading.

We have used *Weird Wambo* for this activity. Write these sentences on the board or copy them and cut them out. The pupils should then rewrite them in the correct order. If the pupils are very weak at English, you could provide a much simpler set of sentences for them to sequence. (Note: as before, if you do not have access to this particular reader, rest assured that all the elements do add up!)

> Wambo told Ole her sad story.
>
> Diane saw Ole in the hole. The children tried to get him out but they couldn't.
>
> The children threw stones at Wambo and yelled at her.
>
> Wambo poked her head out of the hole in the tree and asked Diane what had happened to her friend.
>
> Wambo went to tell the children's parents where they were.

Wambo took the children back to the baobab tree.

The children from the village went to play hide and seek in the bush.

Wambo made an ointment for Ole's injured leg and then she bandaged it.

Diane noticed the baobab tree and decided to get help from Wambo.

The other children hid.

Diane went to the tree to find Wambo and ask for her help.

Diane asked Wambo how she came to live by herself.

Diane found a neat garden and animals behind the wall.

Diane shut her eyes and counted.

Diane saw a light flickering inside the tree and called for Wambo. There was no answer.

Wambo gave the children blankets and most of them soon fell asleep.

Ole was screaming for help.

The children hugged Ole then they hugged Wambo.

The children looked for Ole but they couldn't find him.

Diane shouted again and told Wambo they needed her help.

Wambo cooked a meal for the children and made them a hot drink.

Ole shouted that he had fallen down a hole and hurt his leg.

Wambo went with Diane and helped Ole out of the hole using a rope.

Language skills

The JAWS readers can be used to teach about punctuation and grammar. Grammar includes all the main parts of speech – verbs, nouns, adjectives, adverbs, pronouns and so on – as well as direct and indirect speech and different tenses. The activities here are for practice, so your pupils will need some knowledge before they try these exercises.

Punctuation , . ? ! " " “ ” ' ' ‘ ’

Punctuation helps us to make sense of the written word. Commas, full stops, question marks, exclamation marks and speech marks (inverted commas) are all punctuation marks. Inverted commas can be printed differently in different books. In the JAWS readers a (‘) is used at the start of direct speech and a (’) at the end. This book uses these symbols (' ') at the beginning and end of direct speech. Both of these are correct, as are double inverted commas (" ") or (“ ”). It does not matter which style pupils use but they must be consistent.

JAWS readers provide a useful way of looking at how punctuation marks are used. As one exercise, ask pupils to find a page with punctuation marks in *The Frightened Thief* and talk about how and why they are used. You could also ask a pupil to read a page aloud and make sounds or gestures to indicate punctuation marks (e.g. stamping a foot to indicate a full stop). The rest of the class could try to guess which punctuation marks the pupil is indicating.

As a written exercise, ask pupils to punctuate the sentences below. (Remind pupils that punctuation includes the correct use of capital letters as well as punctuation marks.)

- amanor stopped looked around and ran down the street
- where have you been asked mrs kanor
- leave me alone shouted amanor

Verbs

Verbs are those parts of speech which indicate an action. Once pupils know what a verb is, they can choose one verb from the reader and mime it (act it out in silence) for their group. The group has to guess the verb.

From *Weird Wambo* they could choose 'yell', 'forgot', 'noticed' or 'poked', for example; while from *The Frightened Thief* they could choose 'sold', 'cleaned', 'grabbed' or 'punish'.

You can also read out sections of the stories and ask the pupils to put up their hands or shout 'Verb!' whenever you read out a verb.

Tenses

Pupils need to understand that there are different tenses, and that the verb changes according to the tense used. One way of demonstrating this is to ask questions which require answers in different tenses. For example, using *The Frightened Thief*:

- **(Present) What is Amanor doing at the cupboard?**
- **(Past) What did Amanor do at the cupboard?**
- **(Future) What will Amanor do at the cupboard?**

You can also choose sentences and paragraphs from the story and get pupils to change the tense. They can do this orally before they write it in their books. The more practice they get, the easier they will find it.

Another way of showing how the form of the verb changes is to choose a section of the story, and ask the pupils to make a list of the verbs in that section. Let them write the tense next to each verb. Then ask them to change the verbs to another tense. The following example is taken from *Weird Wambo*:

- **forgot (past): forget (present)**
- **wait (present): waited (past)**

- took (past): take (present)
- told (past): tell (present)
- know (present): knew (past)

You could also show your pupils the two different forms of past and present tenses, for example:

Present tense	Past tense
eats, is eating	ate, was eating
calls, is calling	called, was calling
happens, is happening	happened, was happening
cries, is crying	cried, was crying

Proper nouns

Proper nouns are written with an initial capital letter. They are the particular names of people, places or things. Common nouns are the general names, and are written with an initial small letter.

Once pupils have been taught what a proper noun is, they could be asked to find examples in the reader. It may be useful to give them different categories or groups to help them. They could do the following activity in their workbooks. Some words from *The Frightened Thief* have been filled in as examples.

Group	Proper noun
first names	Amanor
surnames	Peku
cities	Accra
shop names	Victory Grocery
street names	Tiptoe Gardens

Dictionary work

If pupils learn to use a dictionary properly, their study of English is made far easier. We have found it useful to ask the pupils to look up the meaning of certain words in the glossary at the back of the reader. They use a dictionary to look up the same words. An activity like this one may follow, taken from *The Frightened Thief*:

Words to find: kiosk, pliers, traffic lights

- What do these words mean?
- Draw a picture to show what each word means.
- Write down words in another language which mean the same as these words.
- Does the glossary in the reader give you the same meaning as the dictionary? Discuss any differences between the two.

If no dictionary is available, pupils can use the glossary only or talk to older pupils and parents. You should encourage your pupils to try to work out what a word means before telling them.

Writing skills

Writing skills allow pupils to express themselves in a variety of ways. The skills they practise in school can be useful to them in real life. Writing activities also allow pupils to gain a deeper understanding of the books they read. Writing lessons need to be carefully structured, especially if the pupils are not used to writing. You cannot expect perfect work immediately but, with help and motivation, all children can improve their writing skills.

Writing a note

A note is a short, informal letter. Notes are written to give people a message. People write notes to excuse themselves from school or work, to say where they have gone, to ask questions or to give each other information. Look at the example on the next page.

Tuesday

Mother

I bought the bread and tomatoes, but I forgot to get the sugar. Sorry. I'll go back after school.

See you later.

Michael

You could get your pupils to write a note excusing themselves from a lesson. Once they understand how to write a note, they can pretend to be Amanor in *The Frightened Thief* and write a note of apology to Miss Peku.

Filling in a form

Collect forms which people might need to complete in your area: school registration forms, application forms, clinic forms, etc. Show these forms to the pupils and discuss the purpose of each one. (It is interesting to look at forms in different languages and to compare them.)

Let the pupils draw up a form of their own. For example, referring to *The Frightened Thief*, they could draw up a form that Miss Peku would need to fill in, reporting the incident with Amanor. (This would need to include a heading, spaces or boxes for the names of the school, the teacher, the pupil, the date, signature of teacher, a description of the incident itself, and anything else the pupils think relevant.)

You could also copy the hospital accident report form set out on page 22, and get the pupils to complete it. (This activity is often best done in pairs or groups.) They should imagine they are the doctor who treated Amanor after his accident. The information required can be found in the story.

A27B

ACCRA STATE HOSPITAL

Accident Report

Patient's name: ______________________________

Age: ______________________________________

Relative to contact: __________________________

Contact number or address: ____________________

____

Nature of injuries: ____________________________

____

____

Notes: _____________________________________

____

Signature of doctor: ______________ Date: _______

Writing a rhyming chant

You can encourage your pupils' imagination and creativity by getting them to make up a rhyming chant. It might be useful to introduce this idea by referring to African songs which pupils know in their own language. In this way, you can draw attention to sounds and rhyming words in a familiar context.

As an example, and using *Weird Wambo*, the pupils could pretend they are village children and write a chant to shout at Wambo.

- The pupils work in groups.
- Ask the pupils to shout out some words which are insulting or hurtful to Wambo.

- Then ask them to find words which rhyme. For example, 'rat' rhymes with 'bat' and 'cat', 'trees' rhymes with 'fleas', etc. This is quite a fun activity on its own.
- Let each group choose some of the rhyming words and write a chant. This is what one group wrote:

  Wambo Wambo
  lives in the trees, all alone and full of fleas
  ugly like a vampire bat
  eating like a hungry rat.

- After the groups have chanted their rhymes, it might be good to discuss how Wambo felt when she heard them.

Writing a summary

Read the back cover of the book, where the story is described. This kind of summary is called a 'blurb'. It does not tell the full story, but it gives enough information to encourage the children to read further. The blurb for *Weird Wambo* reads:

> Weird Wambo lives all alone
> in a baobab tree. The children of the village
> laugh at her and throw stones.
> But one day something happens
> and they need her help …

The blurb for *The Frightened Thief* reads:

> Amanor must find money to give to the school bullies.
> He is very frightened.
> What can he do to get it?

Each blurb contains only a few sentences. It would be useful to let the pupils discuss which parts of the action in the story are summarised in the blurb. You could also ask how a question in the blurb could encourage the reader to find out more about the book. And what about the use of dot-dot-dot at the end of a blurb? This is supposed to intrigue the readers, make them want to find out more – does this work for your pupils?

- Let the pupils make up the names of some stories. (You could also use some of the other Level 1 titles on page 87.)
- The pupils then choose one of the story names and write a back cover blurb.

Producing a comic strip

The pupils can rewrite the story of, say, *Weird Wambo* in comic strip form. The pupils should be divided into small groups or pairs. Each group is given a few pages of the story to work with.

Here is an example of a comic strip for pages 1–3.

- Each incident is drawn in a frame.
- Pictures are drawn to show what is happening or what is being said.
- The things that are said in the strip are placed in speech bubbles. The speech bubbles are also useful for reinforcing and teaching punctuation and direct speech.
- A line or two of the story may be written at the bottom of the frame to describe the action.

It is useful to get the groups to work in frames which are the same size. Then, when the comics are finished, they can be pasted into a book.

Paragraph writing

Before trying activities like this one, the pupils need to know what a paragraph is. The idea that a paragraph is a group of sentences which deal with one topic can be taught using the readers. Pupils can look at different paragraphs in the story and see how they are structured and punctuated. They can also identify the main topic of each paragraph, i.e. what is the paragraph about?

Once pupils are familiar with the idea of a paragraph they could write their own paragraphs. For example, ask them to write a paragraph that continues the story of *Weird Wambo*: it should describe how the adults in the village react when Wambo tells them that their children are safe at her tree house.

Integration

The Frightened Thief

Maths

Amanor's parents both own shops. Amanor helps them by adding up prices and giving change. You could give your pupils maths problems related to the story. For example: Mrs Djoletu buys 2 sandwiches at [?] each, 1 packet of flour which costs [?] and two drinks which are [?] each. How much will she have to pay altogether? How much change will she get if she pays with [?]? (Use your local currency and make sure prices are appropriate.)

Health

Amanor's parents both sell snacks. Some snacks are healthy, others are not. Pupils can cut pictures of food from magazines or draw pictures from books. They combine their pictures to make posters showing foods which are good for us, and foods which are not so healthy. A class discussion can take place around the posters and the issue of a balanced and healthy diet.

Life skills

Role play

Two pupils are taken aside and given instructions for the role play (acting out). They are to pretend to be two people who are insulting each other and calling each other rude names. They act this out in front of the class. The pupils then talk about why people insult each other, how it feels to be insulted and what the correct way of handling insults might be.

Discussion

You can re-read the section where Amanor is caught stealing and where he runs away. The pupils discuss questions like:

- **Why did he steal the money?**
- **What could he have done instead of stealing?**
- **What do you think you would have done if you had been in the same situation?**

Encourage the pupils to apply what they learn to their own lives. In this way, they can learn to make their own decisions.

Moral issues

Many JAWS titles in Level 1 teach the reader a lesson, for example *Trolley Trouble*, *The Big Fight*, *Caught in the Act* and *The Paper Chase*. Divide the class into groups and ask them to choose one of these titles to read. The groups then tell the rest of the class what moral issues they read about.

The class could draw up a table comparing the issues which the characters face, and the solutions they choose.

Weird Wambo

Health education

Ask the pupils to find out about traditional medicine in their own country. Encourage them to ask local people, collect information and complete a table like this:

Medicine	Purpose
potato skins	bandages for burns

You could also arrange for a herbalist to visit the class and talk to the pupils about natural medicines.

Art

Collect posters which have social messages – posters about AIDS, health posters, political posters, etc. Have a class discussion about the posters. Which ones do the pupils like? Why? Which ones are clearest and easiest to read? Why? How is information shown/given on the posters?

Point out to the pupils that the best posters have a short, catchy slogan and very clear artwork which is usually bright and eye-catching. Then let them work together to design and draw a poster about respecting other people. The posters can be displayed around the school.

Look at the front cover of *Weird Wambo* (and other titles). Let the pupils design another cover for the book.

Life skills

Role play situations of people showing disrespect for each other. For example, disrespect to an older person, to friends, to teachers.

Set questions which can be discussed afterwards:

- Why were the people in the plays being disrespectful?
- What do your parents think is disrespectful? Do you always agree with them?
- How do people show respect for each other?
- Why is it important to respect other members of the community?

Diane and the other children play a game called hide and seek in the story. Let the pupils demonstrate a game that they play and give oral instructions and rules for playing.

4 Activities for Level 2

At Level 2, pupils should be more fluent and confident in English. In this section we will present a wide variety of activities which once again focus on the main areas of language development.

We have selected two titles: *Mr Kalogo's Factory* by Paulinos Vincent Magombe and *The Picture That Came Alive* by Hugh Lewin. Again, though, you should feel free to try the activities with any Level 2 title.

SYNOPSES

Mr Kalogo's Factory is set in Uganda, in a small, beautiful village called Kyenyanja. Mafabi is the young son of the village chief, Gidongo. One day, a large, loud man called Mr Kalogo visits the village; he works in the Department of Rural Development, and announces that a paper factory will be built in the village. This provokes furious protest: the villagers fear damage to the environment. They hold a meeting, at which Kalogo puts the case for jobs and money. But Gidongo tells the people about another paper factory that Mr Kalogo was involved in; it caused terrible pollution and people died. Mr Kalogo is chased from the village, and gives up his plan. The villagers rejoice.

The Picture That Came Alive is set in South Africa. A young village girl, Thoko, tells the story of a picture of a man with a lovely smile. Her father brings it home and hangs it on the wall. When a policeman tells him he shouldn't have the picture, Thoko's father hides it.

Thoko finds out that the man in the picture has been imprisoned for twenty-six years; his 'crime' was fighting for the people's freedom. One day Thoko hears that the man has been freed; everyone rejoices. Then comes the news that the man will come to Thoko's village. After a long wait, he does indeed pay them a visit, to everybody's joy. He even kisses Thoko, who will always remember this great day, 'when the picture came alive'. (NB: The story does not actually mention Nelson Mandela by name, but it is obviously about him.)

Using both readers, we have focused on the following skills and suggested relevant activities. (They follow on from those suggested for Level 1, sometimes enlarging a topic, sometimes introducing a new area of application.)

Oral skills

- questioning
- group discussions
- giving a speech
- role play
- poetry reading

Reading skills

- multiple-choice comprehension
- distinguishing cause and effect
- analysing setting and plot
- collecting related newspaper articles
- identifying the author's intentions

Language skills

- direct speech
- contractions
- adjectives
- figurative language – similes

Writing skills

- writing newspaper reports
- praise poetry
- shape poems

- 'spelling' poems
- slogans
- memorandums

Oral skills

As with some activities for Level 1, these may involve written work too; but again, the emphasis is on oral expression.

Questioning

It is a useful exercise to ask the pupils questions about the cover of a book before you begin to read it. This allows them to interpret pictures and make predictions about the story. Encourage them to express opinions and observations whether they are correct or not.

Looking at the cover of *Mr Kalogo's Factory*, you could start by making sure that the pupils can identify the book title and the name of the author. Then ask them questions like:

- **Does this story take place in the city or in a rural area?**
- **Who do you think the man with the black hat is?**
- **Why are the people protesting?**
- **Why do you think the man in the white shirt has his arms folded?**
- **What does the title tell you about the story?**

Since pupils have already learned about 'blurbs' (the summaries on the back cover of the book, see page 23), you could also encourage them to make predictions based on their reading of the blurb here:

Mr Kalogo comes to Kyenyanja to build a new factory. He tells the people it will bring jobs and money to the village. But the people are against his plan. Their chief knows that Mr Kalogo has a terrible secret. It is a secret which could destroy the village.

Once the children have read a story, then of course you can base your questions on the text. After reading *The Picture That Came Alive*, explain to the pupils that President Mandela really did visit a school, Orange Grove Primary School, in Johannesburg, South Africa. Ask them questions like:

- How do you think Orange Grove School prepared for the President's visit?
- How do you think the pupils and teachers felt about the visit?
- What questions do you think the pupils asked the President?
- If a famous person visited your school, what would you ask him or her?

Group discussions

When questions have encouraged the pupils to think in depth about a story, you can structure group discussions about aspects of it. For example, taking *Mr Kalogo's Factory*, the pupils could consider the state of their own environment.

In groups, the pupils record what their own environment is like. They also discuss how people have affected the environment around them. Each group should suggest solutions to one or two of the problems which they identify. The main points of their discussion should be recorded in a spray diagram like the one opposite.

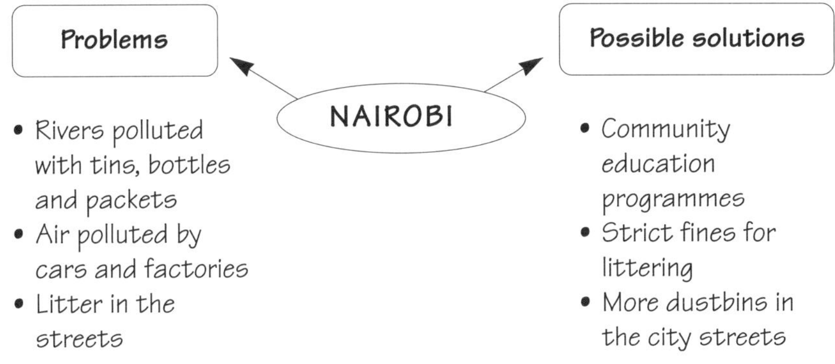

After the groups have finished their discussions, they can use their diagrams to report back to the rest of the class.

Giving a speech

It is a very useful exercise for pupils to research a topic and prepare a speech on it. For example, after reading *The Picture That Came Alive*, the pupils should collect as much information as possible on Nelson Mandela. They can find this in history books, newspapers and from older people. They then use this material to prepare a short talk about President Mandela.

- You should give the pupils some headings to guide them. For example: early history, prisoner, Mandela today.
- Pupils should write down keywords to help them remember their speech, and practise saying it. Then they can say it for the class.

Role play

In this activity, the pupils take on the character of people in the story, in a question-and-answer session. For example, inspired by *The Picture That Came Alive*, each pupil could prepare questions which he or she would ask Nelson Mandela. One pupil, or you yourself, could play the role of Mandela and answer the questions.

Poetry reading

This activity assumes that the pupils will already have had some teaching about the structure and forms of poetry.

Reading poetry aloud is a great aid in vocal expression for the pupils, while writing their own poems encourages imagination and creativity.

The environmental theme of *Mr Kalogo's Factory* can encourage your pupils to focus on poetry about the natural world in general. As an example, we reproduce below 'The Winterman' by Lionel Murcott.

The Winterman's coming.
With his thin blue feet
he walks the lawn white.
With his long grey fingers
he taps the trees
and down fall their leaves.
He stalks through the land,
breathes out cloudless cold air.

Until the Spring-girl catches him.

She ties him up
with ropes of green,
shoves him headfirst down an old antbear hole,
kicks in sand
and stamps and packs it tight.

Blossom and cloud
hang white.

The sun swings longer,
higher.

And he lies underground
with his eyes open,
with sand in his eyes,
and strains at his bonds.

The ropes turn yellow.
The ropes turn red,
they burst apart.

The Winterman claws his way out of the ground.

He shakes the trees
with his long grey hands.
He walks
with thin blue feet
through the land.

There are many anthologies which include poems about the environment. You could select poems and ask pupils to read them aloud to the class.

Once the pupils have read the poems, they can write a few lines explaining what the poem meant to them. You could also encourage the pupils to write their own poetry about the natural world, and read it aloud.

Reading skills

Multiple-choice comprehension

Multiple-choice questions are a useful variation of the comprehension exercise given on page 13. They allow you to assess comprehension quickly and easily. Pupils benefit because they learn to read critically and decide which answer is correct.

You should set multiple-choice tests so that all options are possible, but only one is correct. It is useful to have three options, where possible: one correct, one close to correct, and one which is clearly wrong (if the pupil has understood the story). How the pupils answer the questions depends on how you present the test – they can underline the correct answer or write it down from the chalkboard.

Using *Mr Kalogo's Factory*, you could phrase questions in the following way. (Again, if you do not have access to this particular reader, rest assured that the answer is clear in the text.)

1 The village of Kyenyanja is on the banks of the River:
  a Nile
  b Zambezi
  c Chuene

2 Mr Kalogo works for the Department of:
  a Water
  b Land Affairs
  c Rural Development

3 Mr Kalogo wants to build a factory to make:
  a clothes
  b paper
  c motor vehicles

4 Chief Gidongo doesn't want the factory to be built because:
  a he is a selfish man
  b he wouldn't get any money from it
  c he is concerned about the damage it would cause

5 When Mr Kalogo returns to the village he is very surprised because:
  a the people want to build the factory
  b the people are protesting
  c another factory has been built

6 Mr Kalogo tries to convince the people that:
  a they will get jobs and land when the factory is built
  b they will all have to move
  c their chief is being unfair

7 When Chief Gidongo asks Mr Kalogo to tell the people about the factory in Nampanga, Mr Kalogo:
  a tells them about it
  b does not want to tell them
  c says the chief is lying

8 When some of the protesters become violent, the chief:
   a tells them to kill Mr Kalogo
   b tells them not to use violence
   c leaves the village in disgust
9 The paper factory:
   a will be built in the village
   b will not be built in the village

Distinguishing cause and effect

Cause-and-effect exercises help the pupils to understand what causes incidents or events, and what happens as a result of them. The concept of cause and effect is particularly important in the study of history.

For example, Vusi does badly at school, so his parents forbid him to play soccer. Doing badly is the cause. The effect is that he cannot play soccer.

Create activities from JAWS readers to practise identifying cause and effect. For example, in *The Picture That Came Alive*, ask the pupils to describe the effect of each of the following incidents:

- Nelson Mandela is released from prison.
- Thoko's father has a picture of Nelson Mandela on the wall.
- When President Mandela arrives, he sees the children.

Analysing setting and plot

The setting of a story is where it takes place. Settings can be real or imagined. The plot is the chain of events in the story – what happens.

After reading a story, encourage the pupils to analyse the setting and plot. They can complete a spray diagram like the one below, based on *The Picture That Came Alive*, to demonstrate their understanding.

Collecting related newspaper articles

Once pupils have understood the theme of a story, they could collect related articles from newspapers (if they have access to them). For example, inspired by *Mr Kalogo's Factory*, let them collect articles about the environment. There are often articles about oil spills, earthquakes, pollution, destruction of wildlife and so on in the papers.

Pupils should share their articles with the rest of the class by highlighting the main points. The articles can then be displayed in the classroom so pupils can read them in more detail.

Identifying the author's intentions

The aim of this exercise is to make pupils aware that all writing has a purpose, even trivial-seeming notes. For example, we would write a shopping list to remind ourselves what to buy, or a letter to someone to tell them some news.

In groups, let the pupils discuss Paulinos Vincent Magombe's intentions in writing *Mr Kalogo's Factory*. What do they think he hoped to achieve?

Encourage the pupils to comment on the story themselves. You could start them thinking by asking questions such as:

- **What did you like in the story?**
- **What did you not like about the story?**
- **What have you learned from the story?**

Language skills

Direct speech

Direct speech refers to the exact words spoken by somebody. It is usually accompanied by the 'reporting verb' ('said', etc.). Direct speech is written in speech marks – single quotes (' ') or double (" "). (You may like to advise your pupils which style they should follow in school work. See also page 17.)

The speech in the picture above could be written as:

- **'I'm very pleased to visit your village,' said President Mandela.**
- **'Viva President Mandela!' shouted Thoko.**

Let the pupils find and read examples of direct speech in both the stories. They could use these to list rules for writing direct speech (especially where to place the punctuation).

Allow pupils to practise writing direct speech. Give them some sentences showing indirect reporting, and ask them to rewrite them in direct speech. For example:

- **The policeman told him to take down the picture. (The policeman told him, 'Take down the picture.')**

- **Thoko told everyone she was really excited.**
  ('I'm really excited,' Thoko told everyone.)
- **A small boy shouted that Mandela was coming.**
  ('Mandela is coming!' shouted a small boy.)

Contractions

Contractions are shortened forms of words or phrases. An apostrophe replaces the missing letters. For example:

- they are = they're
- do not = don't
- I will = I'll
- they had = they'd
- we have = we've

Contractions are perfectly acceptable in modern spoken and written English.

As an exercise, show your pupils the following sentences (taken from *The Picture That Came Alive*), and ask them first to identify the contraction, and then give the full meaning of each of them.

- **I'd remember fishing in the pools.**
- **He didn't look surprised or scared.**
- **'But I'll always remember today,' I said.**
- **'That's older than Mandla's father who works in the mines.'**

Adjectives

An adjective describes a noun.

Read extracts from *Mr Kalogo's Factory* and ask pupils to write down any adjectives they hear. You could also write down a summary from the story, leaving gaps for the pupils to fill with any appropriate adjectives (but not the ones from the story!).

Kyenyanja is a _____ village. The _____ villagers lived there for many generations. Their ______ chief had ruled for many years.

Figurative language – similes

A simile is a figure of speech that compares one thing to another. For example, Mr Kalogo in the story is 'as silent as a stone'.

Let the pupils draw a picture to illustrate this. If they enjoy the activity they can find more similes in their readers and illustrate them as well. (See the example below.)

He was as big as a house!

Pupils can complete similes by supplying their own endings. This kind of exercise helps their creative writing and teaches them about figures of speech. For example:

- Gidongo was as firm as ...
- The villagers were as angry as ...
- Mr Kalogo was as frightened as ...

Writing skills

Writing newspaper reports

Newspaper reports need to be short and simple to get their message across to readers. This activity encourages pupils to express themselves clearly and briefly.

Newspaper reports are usually modelled on the example given here (the numbers are keyed into the example).

A New Beginning

Nkanyiso Mthemba
Johannesburg Bureau

This is Itumeleng's first day at Parkhurst Primary School. He is looking forward to meeting his teacher and his fellow pupils.

He is particularly excited because he hopes to join the police force one day and knows he will need to study hard to achieve this.

The dream begins for Itumeleng

1. Reports always have a **headline**. Headlines are short headings given to articles.
2. The articles are divided into **paragraphs**.
3. Often **photographs** are included.
4. A **caption** next to the photograph tells the reader what it is.
5. The name of the **journalist** who wrote the article is usually printed under the headline or at the end of the report.

Get the pupils to make up a newspaper report about Mr Kalogo's failed attempt to have a factory built in Kyenyanja. (They could use a drawing instead of the photograph.)

Praise poetry

It is an African tradition to write and sing praises to honoured leaders. Here is an example:

Viva Mandela!
God bless our president
the father of our freedom
the leader of our nation.
Praise to he who is full of love and mercy
the heart of our nation.

Let the pupils write and perform praise poems to a respected leader in your own country.

Shape poems

These are set out in such a way that the lines form a shape related to the topic of the poem. Show the pupils examples of shape poems like the one here. Get them to draw a shape and write their own shape poems within it – this can be a particularly challenging exercise. *Mr Kalogo's Factory* may inspire shapes like a tree, or a factory.

6
5, 4,
3, 2, 1,
Blast off!
Engines roar
as the tower
of steel begins
to rise. Man,
to achieve
an earthly
dream, confronts
the greatest
dangers ever
known. The force
of gravity overcome,
the rocket speeds
onwards towards the
waiting
Moon.

'Spelling' poems

These poems also reflect their topic in a special way. Here, the first letters of all the lines spell it out. In the example below, the word is MUSIC.

Memories, moving
Uplifting, ubiquitous
Soothing and spiritual
International and inspiring
Classical and creative.

Let the pupils create their own poems with the name MANDELA (or the name of a leader in their own country).

Slogans

A slogan is a short precise statement, which aims to send a particular message. The banners on the cover of *Mr Kalogo's Factory* have some slogans on them.

The pupils can pretend they are the people in the story. Each pupil should write a slogan for a banner and show it to the class. The class can choose the best five, and say why they liked these.

Memorandums

Make sure the pupils understand what a memorandum (memo) is: a short written notice. You could write an example on the board:

> **MEMO**
>
> To: The teachers of Happy Valley School
>
> From: The pupils of Happy Valley School
>
> We are having a problem in the playground. The pupils from the other school are coming into the playground and bullying us. The prefects are too small to do anything about this. Please could you do something to help.
>
> Thank you

Let the pupils write a memo from Mr Kalogo to the government officials. In his memo he is complaining about the behaviour of the villagers.

Integration

Mr Kalogo's Factory

Art

Pupils fold a piece of paper in half. On one half they draw a clean healthy environment. On the other half, they draw the same environment being polluted.

Pupils could also draw anti-litter posters and display them around the school.

Geography

The people in the story don't want the factory. What could they do to earn a living without the factory? The pupils make a list of the things people can do to earn money and survive. For example: farming, making drinks from local products, weaving, building or repairing tools, working in health care, selling crafts.

General science

Pupils work in pairs and write down the causes of different types of pollution, as in the example started here.

Air pollution	Water pollution	Land pollution
1. Cars	1. Chemicals	1. Litter
2.	2.	2.
3.	3.	3.
4.	4.	4.

The Picture That Came Alive

History

African countries have had many struggles for liberation and independence.

Ask the pupils to choose a leader from their own country. The person they choose should have contributed in some way to independence or liberation struggles.

The pupils should write a profile of the leader they have chosen. They may need to do some further reading or research to find information.

Leader Profile

Name of leader:

Country:

Contribution to the liberation
struggle in Africa:

Projects

The pupils find out about the liberation struggles of their own country. They present the information in the form of a short project. They could draw a poster, present a talk show or write their information as an interview.

5 Activities for Level 3

At this level, pupils are expected to read more, and to cope with more complicated language and structure. By now, they should be fairly competent at English. Accordingly, there are fewer pictures in the JAWS readers to help them.

We have selected two titles: *The Haunted Taxi Driver* by Kofi Sekyi and *Tikrit* by Chris Burchell. Unlike the previous two levels, we consider these two titles separately, and *Tikrit* is singled out as a practical example of how to use a JAWS reader in a plan of work for English. We give more details on page 58.

SYNOPSIS

The Haunted Taxi Driver is set in Ghana. Baba Oko, a 26-year-old taxi driver, drives into a young girl one night when he has drunk too much beer. Oko thinks he has killed her, and drives away in panic. He hides for two months, then feels safe to go back to his normal life. But he seems to be haunted by the hideous ghost of the young girl: wherever he goes he sees her. In despair, he runs to a police station to confess his crime, but the ghost even follows him there. It turns out to be the brother of the girl, in a fright mask; he recognised Oko driving away from the scene of the accident. His sister survived, but he swore to get his revenge on the guilty driver. Oko vows never to drink and drive again.

We have focused on the following skills and suggested relevant activities. They follow on from those suggested for

Levels 1 and 2, again sometimes reinforcing a topic, sometimes introducing a new area of application. They are designed to encourage even more confidence and to develop fluency and other language skills.

Oral skills
- analysing the book's cover
- memorising details
- introductions
- discussions and debates

Reading skills
- how punctuation works

Language skills
- vocabulary
- similes

Writing skills
- invitations
- spray diagrams
- using the senses
- advertisements

Oral skills

Analysing the book's cover

As with the exercise on page 31, encourage your pupils to look closely at the cover of the book and think about the details. Ask them questions like:

- What is the meaning of the title?
- What do you think the book is about?

- Look at the people on the cover. What do you think about them, before you know the story?
- Look at the expressions on those people's faces. Try to make the expressions yourself. How do you think the people are feeling?
- Are you looking forward to reading the story? Why?

You can use this technique to get pupils to talk about what they see and think about all the books they read.

Memorising details

This exercise, a memory game, encourages the pupils to be more observant, improves and reinforces new vocabulary, and improves memory skills.

You can use the cover or any inside illustration to do this exercise. Pupils can play the memory game in pairs or small groups.

Rules of the game

- Give the pupils a limited time to look carefully at the picture they have chosen.
- Tell them to memorise all the details they can.
- Close the book or remove the picture and ask them to describe the picture accurately.
- Afterwards they can look back at the picture to see how much they remembered.

Variations

You can play a memory game with text as well: read an extract from the story and get the pupils to listen carefully for nouns, or adjectives, or other parts of speech. At the end of the extract, they list all those that they can remember.

For fun, you can ask them to listen to the extract and remember all the words starting with 'S' (or any other letter). They are not allowed to write while you are reading. They may only memorise mentally.

You can also read an extract, then write down key phrases from the reading. Write the phrases down in a haphazard order and give the pupils copies. Then, in an exercise similar to that on page 15, ask them to sequence the phrases in the correct order.

Introductions

The JAWS stories are full of interesting characters in a range of settings. As each story progresses, we are introduced to new characters and we learn more about the earlier ones.

We may find out about a character's:

- age
- occupation
- physical appearance
- personality
- interests

Get the pupils to introduce themselves to the class. They can use the headings above as guidelines. You can also ask pupils to introduce a friend or a family member, real or imagined. For example, here is a pupil introducing a family member:

Good morning, class. I'd like to introduce you to my grandmother. She is 87 years old and she is a herbalist. You will notice that she walks with a white stick – this is because her eyes are failing. However, she is still independent and healthy and she likes to walk in the forest and collect herbs to make medicine. She identifies the herbs and plants by feel and smell.

Once the pupils have read the JAWS stories they can practise introducing characters from the book.

Discussions and debates

We have already introduced various methods of starting discussions. A debate is a more formal, structured discussion where two different points of view are presented. The audience listens to each point of view and then decides which one they agree with. First you need to choose a chairperson. The chairperson makes sure that everyone sticks to the rules.

The rules of classroom debates are:

- Each person has the same amount of time to speak.
- The audience should listen attentively and may not interrupt.
- Speakers should speak briefly and stick to the topic.
- After each person has spoken, the chairperson may allow a few questions from the audience.
- If anybody disagrees with a speaker, he or she may say so, but must give reasons for their point of view.

Topics for debates should be controversial. For example you could have a debate on whether or not people should be allowed to drive at the age of fifteen. Or, you could debate whether or not smoking should be allowed at school. Referring to *The Haunted Taxi Driver*, you could debate whether people should drink alcohol if they are going to drive.

Reading skills

How punctuation works

As we mentioned earlier (page 17), punctuation marks help readers to understand what is written. Without punctuation, it could be difficult to work out the meaning of a sentence. You can make this point by writing a paragraph from one of the books on the board with absolutely no punctuation. Ask the pupils to read it. Discuss why it is difficult to understand, and explain the function of each punctuation mark, here concentrating on:

? (question mark) shows that something is being asked
. (full stop) indicates the end of a sentence or an abbreviation
, (comma) indicates a pause
! (exclamation mark) signals a strong feeling or a shouted command
' ' or **" "** (inverted commas) indicate that someone is speaking (see the activity on direct speech on page 39).

Ask the pupils to find examples of different punctuation marks in the books. Once they have done so, ask them the relevant questions:

- **(for a question mark) What is the answer to the question?**
- **(for a full stop) What is the new sentence about?**
- **(for a comma) Why is it necessary to pause here?**
- **(for an exclamation mark) What feeling is being expressed?**
- **(for inverted commas) Who is talking and to whom?**

Language skills

Vocabulary

One way of increasing vocabulary awareness is by grouping words together when they are associated with the same thing. To give your pupils an example, you could use *The Haunted Taxi Driver* and group the words which are associated with the police station:

- **police station:** inspector, constable, sergeant, notebook, handcuffs, gun, uniform, badge, cap

Pupils could complete similar groupings for the following:

- **family:**
- **punishment:**
- **fear:**
- **hospital:**

Similes

As we said on page 41, similes are comparisons of one thing with another. They make writing more interesting and stimulate the imagination. For example, compare these two sentences:

- Mr Nkebe was afraid.
- Mr Nkebe was as frightened as a rabbit.

The second sentence gives a vivid idea of just how Mr Nkebe was feeling.

Encourage pupils to make up their own similes. This helps them develop language skills and vocabulary. It also makes creative writing more interesting.

You could ask your pupils to complete the following:

- as ______ as a crow
- as ______ as a hippopotamus
- as soft as ______
- as angry as ______

Writing skills

Invitations

On page 20 we looked at writing short informal notes. Invitations are rather more structured because they have to give specific information clearly. Discuss with the class what should be written on an invitation. The following points are usually included:

- who is being invited
- the date of the event

- the place where the event is being held (address)
- the time the event starts and when it will finish
- who is sending the invitation
- the style – whether the event is formal or casual

Share ideas about the design of the invitation – which kind of paper, card or other material to use, which colours, what type of writing, and so on.

Pupils then create an invitation to a school event, such as a dance or a prize-giving ceremony. Some examples are given below. 'RSVP' stands for *respondez s'il vous plaît* (French for 'please answer').

You are invited to
Musa's Graduation
at Lagos University
on Saturday 12 April
at 15.00.
RSVP Simphiwe 012 486-9423

Postcard

Dear Anina
I'm going to Musa's graduation on Saturday too. Shall we meet up and go there together? What about 1 o'clock at the Carlton Centre for lunch? Let me know if you can make it.
Love, David

Letter

Mr and Mrs Dhlamini invite you to celebrate Musa's graduation.

Date: Saturday 12 April
Time: 3 p.m.
Place: Lagos University
Dress: Informal
RSVP: Simphiwe Dhlamini

Card

Spray diagrams

Spray diagrams are useful for note-making and planning. The diagram is structured so that ideas can flow easily and connections can be made.

- The main idea is placed in a central box.
- The sub-ideas are placed in shapes around the main idea.
- Ideas are connected to each other by arrows.

For example:

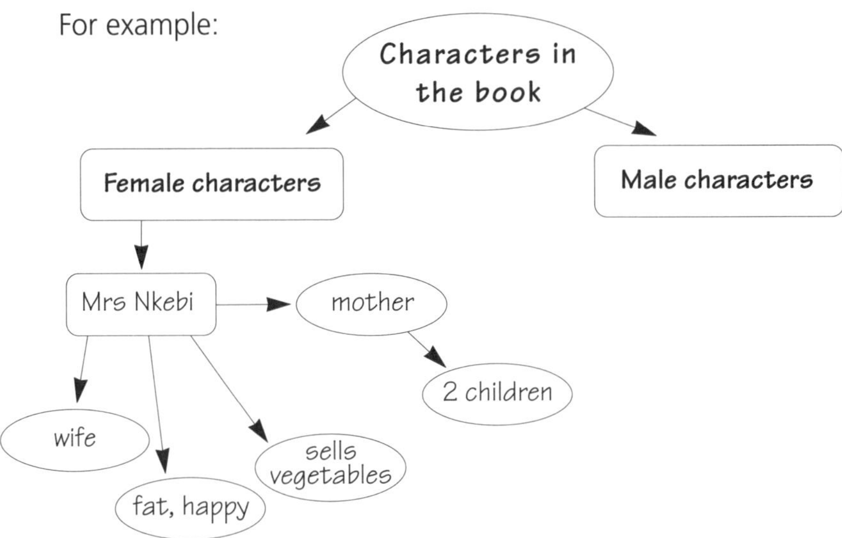

Spray diagrams work well for making notes about characters, exploring emotions and feelings and giving information about places.

Using the senses

Encourage pupils to produce better writing by considering how all five senses experience an event.

For example, take a road accident, like the one in *The Haunted Taxi Driver*, and ask your pupils:

- **Hearing:** what sounds would you hear?
  Screeching, loud bang, thud, tinkling glass, sirens …
- **Smell:** what would you be able to smell?
  Burning rubber from the tyres, petrol …

- **Sight:** what would you see?
  Damaged cars, people staring, blood everywhere …
- **Touch:** what would things physically feel like?
  Sharp pain from wounds, pressure from being crushed …
- **Taste:** would you be aware of tastes?
  There could be blood in your mouth …

Then there are the emotions: how would people feel inside? Weak, dizzy, heart beating rapidly, sick at the sight of blood …

Choose other situations and get pupils to consider what they would hear, smell, see, touch, taste and feel. You could try an argument, a sports event, or being lost in a city.

Advertisements

Adverts are usually:
- clear and easy to read
- informative – telling you what you may want to know about a product
- interesting – they must catch your attention somehow

Get the pupils to design an advertisement for a taxi company. You could put an example on the board to begin the discussion, like the one below.

JETFAST TAXIS

Drivers of sober habits, quick reflexes and skilled driving ability. We will get you there on time and safely.
Call 0294-6421

We're just a moment away …

Integration

The Haunted Taxi Driver

Art

Encourage your pupils to create eye-catching posters.
Some suggested topics:

- don't drink and drive
- a pop-concert
- a circus in town
- a book fair

Life skills

Encourage discussions about:

- career choices – which skills are necessary for manual and non-manual jobs
- sharing feelings and emotions with others
- respecting the culture and beliefs of others

Maths

Bearing in mind the effect of speed in traffic accidents, get the class to investigate the relationship between speed, distance and time. For instance, how long would it take to travel 150 km if your taxi was travelling at 80/100/120 km per hour?

Drama

- Consider the importance of body language – getting across a message without words. What body language do people use when they are frightened/angry/attracted to someone?
- Role play – behaving like another character.

Social studies

Encourage your pupils to research the following points and report their findings to the rest of the class:

- Transport: today we use taxis and buses. How did people travel long distances in the past?
- Alcohol: how does it make people drunk?
- What are the rules of the road in your country?

A work plan using a JAWS reader: *Tikrit*

SYNOPSIS

Tikrit is set in Kenya. Tikrit is a 9-year-old Masai boy. He is always asking questions, which can irritate his elders. But they recognise the boy's intelligence, and his grandfather wishes he had money to pay for his education. One night Tikrit sees fireballs falling to the ground. Nobody believes him, so he goes to where they fell and is frightened off by a flapping parachute. He takes his grandfather to the place, and they find a large camera that has fallen to the ground. They do not realise its value, and try to sell it in Nairobi. But they are secretly followed by some Europeans who want to get the device back. Tikrit and his grandfather are finally confronted by the Europeans, only to find out that there is a reward for finding the special camera (which had been on a satellite). So there is money for school fees for Tikrit.

Using this reader, we developed a two-week work plan. We considered the skills that we needed to teach and wrote down how we would teach them using this book. Here is an example of our work plan.

Theme: *Tikrit* (JAWS Level 3)
Class: senior primary
Duration: 2 weeks, 12 lessons (30 minutes each)

Materials needed:

Tikrit readers

Dictionary (one per group if possible, otherwise one per class)

Skills to be taught	***Techniques and pupil involvement***
Oral Sharing opinions	Pupils to discuss their own opinions about stealing. Discussion to be guided by teacher.
Reading Scanning	Pupils scan text to find proper nouns. These will be used to complete a crossword puzzle (see below). Consider when scanning is useful as a reading technique.
Language Alphabetical order	Pupils look up certain words in the dictionary and write down their meaning.
Writing Questionnaire	Pupils complete a questionnaire by filling in information about themselves as well as about Tikrit (see page 61). They make comparisons afterwards.

A capital crossword puzzle

The pupils will have copies of the crossword which appears on the next page. Tell them that the answers are all proper nouns, the special names given to people, places or things, which start with a capital letter. To answer the clues, they scan the text (read it very quickly), looking for the relevant words, filling in the puzzle as they go. This is a fun way to find and record information – highly adaptable to other exercises.

		1		2						3
4										
				5						
			6							
7										

Across

1 A character in the book who is always asking questions.
4 A strong car, like a jeep (2 words).
5 The capital city of Kenya.
6 Torosei the cousin lives here.
7 The plains where the boy and his grandfather live.

Down

2 The street where the boy and his grandfather meet the stranger.
3 Grandfather belongs to this group of people.
4 The hill where the parachute was found.

Answers

Across 1 Tikrit; 4 Land Rover; 5 Nairobi; 6 Mathare; 7 Athi.
Down 2 Kirinya; 3 Masai; 4 Longata.

Getting to know you: a questionnaire

This is a useful exercise to encourage the pupils to analyse and record information about a character, and, of course, to think about their own lives.

	Character	*Yourself*
Name:	Tikrit	
Age:		
Date of birth (year only):		
Nationality (e.g. Zulu, SA):		
Country of birth:		
Town/City of birth:		
Interests:		
Kind of dwelling (e.g. house, hut, flat):		
Other occupants (i.e. who also live there):		
Their occupation (i.e. the work they do):		

6 Activities for Level 4

At this level, pupils should be competent at using English. The activities can therefore be rather more sophisticated.

Level 4 titles deal with issues of a more adult nature: for example, crime, politics and violence. We have selected *The Innocent Prisoner* by Kwasi Koranteng, which is concerned with drugs and drug dealing, and their effect on young people's lives.

SYNOPSIS

The Innocent Prisoner is set in Ghana. Brakwa is just 21, and is looking forward to going to the USA to study. He buys a suitcase for the journey from a shop in Accra. But he does not realise the shop assistant is a member of a drug smuggling ring; at the airport, the villains swap Brakwa's suitcase for an identical one carrying cocaine. Brakwa is caught, tried and sentenced to ten years' imprisonment. His devastated friends, including his girlfriend Beesiwa, are determined to clear his name. They suspect the suitcase may have been switched, so one friend, Gyan, re-enacts Brakwa's movements, buying a suitcase from the same shop, travelling the same way, and so on. But the villains discover their plan, and imprison another friend, Adane. After much excitement, the friends involve the police and the villains are caught red-handed at the airport.

As you work through this novel with your pupils, you can encourage discussion about personal experiences. You can also ask the pupils to form their own opinions based on careful research and factual knowledge, rather than just emotional responses. Here we have focused on the following skills and activities:

Oral skills
- addressing people

Reading skills
- reading for the main idea
- summarising content
- reading for information

Language skills
- abbreviations
- adjectives and adverbs
- pronouns
- prepositions

Writing skills
- concise language
- writing a letter
- writing a diary

Oral skills

Addressing people

People speak to each other throughout the story.

- The shop assistant says, 'Can I help you?' (page 3)
- Brakwa says, 'Yes, your honour,' in the courtroom. (page 24)
- The court official shouts, 'Silence in court!' (page 26)

It is important for pupils to realise that different situations require different ways of speaking to people. They can discuss the different ways in which they address each other, parents, strangers, teachers and so on. Once they have discussed the different forms of address they use, they can try out some role-play situations in pairs. Some situations to try out are:

- buying goods from a hawker at a market
- asking the time of a flight at an airport
- a policewoman arresting a criminal
- a mother saying goodbye to her child
- a person trying to get his car fixed

The pupils act out the conversations (in any language) between the people in these situations.

Set up a role play where one person is English-speaking and the other is not. Discuss how the situation changes when people try to converse in different languages. How might people who cannot speak a language try to make themselves understood?

Reading skills

Reading for the main idea

Paragraphs, chapters and whole books can be used to identify the main idea. It is useful to start with paragraphs at a lower level of reader and progress to chapters at Level 4.

Pupils need to understand that a chapter has a main idea. The main idea is the gist of what the chapter is about. The rest of the chapter is made up of details. These are the smaller bits of information or facts which help to develop and explain the main ideas. Some details are less important – the story would still work without them.

The following activity is useful for identifying main ideas. We have used Chapter 5, but it can be done with any chapter.

Below are five sentences taken from Chapter 5. The pupils should choose the one which they think describes the main idea of this chapter. In other words, which of these sentences is the most important in Chapter 5?

- **Some people in the courtroom began to laugh.**
- **The judge looked very angry.**
- **'You are guilty of trying to smuggle drugs out of the country.'**
- **'The court sentences you to ten years with hard labour.'**
- **Outside he was not given the chance to say goodbye to his relatives and friends.**

The pupils can work in pairs to select sentences from other chapters. They swap their sentences with other pairs and identify the main ideas.

Pupils can also be asked to write headings for the chapters of the book. The headings should give some indication of the main idea contained in each chapter.

Summarising content

Writing a good summary is an essential study skill. If pupils practise this in English lessons, they will be able to transfer this skill to other subjects more easily.

Once pupils have identified the main idea in each chapter, they can use the information to draw up a summary of the book. A summary briefly describes the story.

Pupils can discuss the difference between a summary of the story and the 'blurb' on the back cover of the book. (See the activity on page 23.) One important difference is that the blurb is intended to 'sell' the book to a prospective reader; it would defeat its own purpose if it gave away too much of the plot.

Similar activities can be done using newspaper articles or films.

Once pupils have completed the summary, they can fill in a worksheet about the book. The information on the worksheet will also help you to see whether they enjoyed the story and how well they managed with the reading. You could use the format suggested below.

Name:

Title of book:

Author:

JAWS level:

What kind of book was it?

What was the book about?

Was the reading easy/just right/difficult/too difficult?

Did you enjoy the book?

Do you think other students of your age will enjoy this book? Give one reason for your answer.

Reading for information

We read for information when we look at timetables, notice boards and road signs. This information is often given in single words, pictures and symbols so that we can find out what we need to know quickly. We tend to ignore the details we do not need. Copy these notices on the board and ask pupils to answer the following questions.

WINDHOEK REGIONAL SERVICES

Floor 1	***Floor 2***
• Security	**• Courtrooms 6 –10**
• Courtrooms 1–5	**• Office of Justice**
• Cafeteria	**• Public telephone**

- On which floor is courtroom 7?
- On which floor is the security checkpoint?
- On which floor would you get a cup of coffee?

TOILETS →

- In which direction would you walk to find the toilets?

- What does this sign mean?

Ask pupils to try to find other common notices or signs in their area. They could draw them on the chalkboard and discuss what they mean with the rest of the class .

Language skills

Abbreviations

Sometimes words are not written out in full, but shortened. Shortened forms are called abbreviations. Abbreviations are normally made up of the initial letters of words, for example: OAU is an abbreviation of The **O**rganisation of **A**frican **U**nity, while Mike is an abbreviation of Michael.

Quite a fun activity is to ask the pupils to make up silly abbreviations for their own names. For example, Si could be short for Kwasi, My could be short for Michael, Mm could be short for Amma and Maa could be short for Mariama. This kind of activity is often the one which pupils remember, and this means that they will remember what an abbreviation is.

Let the pupils scan *The Innocent Prisoner* to find the following abbreviations:

- USA (United States of America)
- Mr (Mister)
- VHF (Very High Frequency)

They should then try to work out what they stand for.

Set the pupils a task. They are to find abbreviations in textbooks, magazines and newspapers and bring them to class with their meanings. Some common examples are:

- **TV (television)**
- **tel (telephone)**
- **PTO (please turn over)**
- **kg (kilogram)**
- **St (street)**
- **NE (North-East)**
- **am (*ante meridiem*, Latin, meaning 'before midday')**
- **UN (United Nations)**

NB: While full stops are commonly used with abbreviations – O.A.U., St. and so on – it is a matter of choice. You should make your pupils aware of the different styles (full stops or no full stops) that they will encounter in different publications. You may wish to make it clear which style they should follow in schoolwork.

Adjectives and adverbs

We have already touched on adjectives (page 40). Adjectives tell us more about nouns (people, places, things). Adverbs tell us more about verbs (actions).

You can choose different parts of speech from the story and place them in categories like this:

Nouns	**Adjectives**
road	thick
suitcase	main
hair	noisy
crowd	blue

Verbs	**Adverbs**
listen	early
leave	inside
stand	carefully

The pupils then match the adjectives to the nouns and the adverbs to the verbs as they appear in the story.

After that, the pupils can make up their own adjectives and adverbs.

Pronouns

Pronouns are used in place of nouns. For example:

- **it** instead of **table**
- **him** instead of **Sipho**
- **hers** instead of **Janet's**
- **them** instead of **Stephen, Ana and Beesiwa**

Find examples in the text where pronouns are used. For example (page 11):

- **Her eyes were deep-set and her skin was smooth.**

Who does 'her' refer to? In this case, the pronoun refers to Naana, one of the drug-smuggling characters.

In order to teach the advantage of using pronouns, ask pupils to read from the story, replacing every pronoun with the name of the person or thing being referred to. This soon becomes very cumbersome and pupils learn that the pronouns make reading and writing easier.

You can also ask the pupils to find or write down examples where pronouns can be confusing. Look at the following:

- **The lamp was on and the table was laid. On it was a lovely pattern.**

In this case, we cannot decide easily whether the lamp or the table is 'it' but we can work it out with some thought. For instance, a lamp is more likely to have a pattern on it than a table. Ask your pupils to try to avoid this sort of confusion in their own writing.

Prepositions

Prepositions are difficult to define exactly. Broadly speaking, a preposition is a word (or a group of words) which connects a noun (or the equivalent of a noun) with the rest of a sentence. Prepositions answer the questions:

- where? (e.g. at, by, in, from, into, on)
- when? (e.g. now, at, for, on)
- how? (e.g. with, instead of, against)

The exercise below is an effective one. The illustration, from page 31, gives visual clues for understanding how the prepositions work. Get your pupils to look at the illustration while reading the sentences (the prepositions are in italics).

- The guard is sitting *under* the tree.
- His gun is *in* his hands.
- The prisoners have stars *on* their uniforms.
- The plants are visible *above* the ground.
- The guard is leaning *against* the tree.
- The prisoners are standing *next to* each other.

The pupils could then look through the story and find examples of the following prepositions:

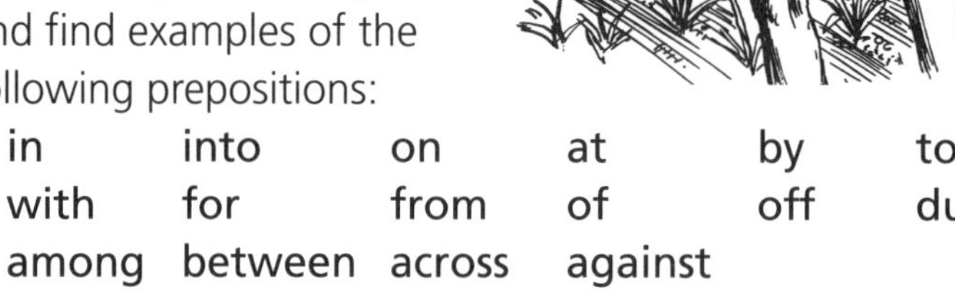

in	into	on	at	by	to
with	for	from	of	off	during
among	between	across	against		

Pupils need practice in choosing and using the correct preposition. Activities like this one can also help. Supply suitable endings for each of these sentences:

- Brakwa decided to look at ______
- Brakwa decided to look for ______
- They walked across ______
- They walked into ______
- We are staying with ______
- We are staying at ______
- Brakwa is waiting in ______
- Brakwa is waiting on ______

Writing skills

Concise language

Sometimes pupils tend to say things in a very long-winded (verbose) manner. We touched on the value of writing clearly and briefly in newspaper reports (page 41).

The chapters in *The Innocent Prisoner* have no headings. Ask the pupils to make up a heading for each chapter, expressing the main idea (see page 64). The chapter heading must be more than ten words long!

Now the pupils swap their chapter headings with each other, and rewrite those long headings using fewer than five words. They must make sure that the meaning stays the same.

Ask your pupils to think about which chapter headings work best, the long ones or the short ones. Why?

Discuss why it is better to write short, clear sentences.

Writing a letter

Being in prison is often terrible for the prisoner and his or her loved ones at home.

Begin this activity by discussing what conditions would be like in prison in your country. Discuss accommodation, food, type of work, and so on.

Ask the pupils to imagine they are in prison (like Brakwa in the story, they're innocent of course!). They should write a letter to someone they care about, a relative or friend. They should express how they are feeling, but remember the prison authorities might read the letter.

The format of the pupils' letters is not important. The focus is on content. Allow them to read their letters to each other.

Writing a diary

There are different types of diary. Personal diaries are a written record of a person's life. In a personal diary people write about what happens to them and how they feel. However, there are also many people who use diaries to organise their time – to keep a record of appointments, special occasions, meetings and things they need to do. Pupils may keep a homework diary, in which they write down their homework every day.

Use the story to develop the skills of diary writing. Give the pupils a diary outline for a week, as follows:

Week number ______ Starts ________ Ends _________	
Monday	Thursday
Tuesday	Friday
Wednesday	Saturday
	Sunday

Pupils choose a character from the story and complete that character's personal diary for the week.

Next, the pupils practise an organising diary. They imagine they are the judge in the story. Complete the diary to show what his week's appointments might look like.

Integration

The Innocent Prisoner

In this case, 'drugs' is taken as a theme, spanning a range of subjects:

- Share any experiences and feelings about drug abuse.
- Find out about different drugs and their effects on people.
- Invite a member of the police force to come and talk to the pupils about drugs.
- Read and cut out newspaper articles about drugs.
- Act out anti-drug plays. Present them to other schools.
- Invite a health care worker to come to school to speak about the effects of drugs.
- Design anti-drug posters.

7 Activities for Level 5

At this level, pupils should be efficient readers. However, it might still be necessary to revise the skills taught earlier, especially if they do not speak or use English regularly. Refer back to the skills grid on pages 6–7 to see which skills you might need to consolidate.

In this section we are going to focus on activities which encourage the pupils to read the books in greater depth. We have selected *Cry Softly, Thule Nene* by Shirley Bojé.

SYNOPSIS

Cry Softly, Thule Nene is set in South Africa. Young Thule Nene's parents have been killed in a savage attack on their village; Thule and her older brother survive. The brother tries to avenge the deaths, and is himself killed, while Thule is taken to a mission run by nuns. Here she works hard and looks after other orphans. After two years, her life changes again when she is invited to help with the crippled young daughter of a rich white family. The girl, Fay Wickham, is spoilt and bitter, but Thule's good heart gradually wins her over. Thule begins to be educated, and life looks promising. But then she pays a visit to the mission, and finds it deteriorating – a sign of general unrest. Violence even comes to the rich white area, and the Wickhams' black housekeeper is killed. Her son, Simon, has grown close to Thule, who loves him. Thule selflessly helps the mission again, aided by the Wickhams. After more trials and misunderstandings, Thule is adopted into the Wickham family and plans a future devoted to helping people as poor and disadvantaged as she once was.

Oral skills

- poetry
- expressing condolences
- themes and issues
- character judgements

Reading skills

- character boxes
- inferential reading

Language skills

- emotive language
- indirect speech
- plurals

Writing skills

- paragraph writing
- letter of condolence
- writing a report
- writing a script

Oral skills

Poetry

'Funeral Blues' by W. H. Auden deals with mourning and sorrow – an appropriate poem to study in relation to *Thule Nene.*

Stop all the clocks, cut off the telephone,
Prevent the dog from barking with a juicy bone,
Silence the pianos and with muffled drum
Bring out the coffin, let the mourners come.

Let aeroplanes circle moaning overhead
Scribbling on the sky the message He Is Dead,

Put crêpe bows round the white necks of the public
doves,
Let the traffic policemen wear black cotton gloves.

He was my North, my South, my East and West,
My working week and my Sunday rest,
My moon, my midnight, my talk, my song;
I thought that love would last for ever: I was wrong.

The stars are not wanted now; put out every one;
Pack up the moon and dismantle the sun;
Pour away the ocean and sweep up the wood;
For nothing now can ever come to any good.

- Divide the class into groups and give them a copy of the poem. Let each group prepare to read the poem aloud to the rest of the class.
- Use the poem to look at the structure of poetry, and to focus on rhyme.
- Let the pupils talk about the poet's feelings and relate them to Thule Nene's feelings when she lost her family. Ask for similarities and differences.
- Use this opportunity to discuss some African funeral dirges as well. This will help to make the experience relevant to the pupils' own backgrounds.

You should try to find other examples of such poems and use them as well.

Expressing condolences

How do different cultures express their sorrow when people die? Have a class discussion around what local people do. This discussion will be more interesting if you have more than one culture and/or religion in your class.

You could ask questions like:
- What behaviour is appropriate for your culture/religion?
- How do different groups express sorrow and mourn the loss of loved ones?

Themes and issues in the book

On page 33 we suggested a spray diagram as a way of recording information. As the pupils read through the book, they can complete diagrams like the one below, recording incidents which relate to the main themes as they occur. Once they have finished the book, they can refer back to the diagrams to discuss the author's intentions (see page 38) and the main themes of the book.

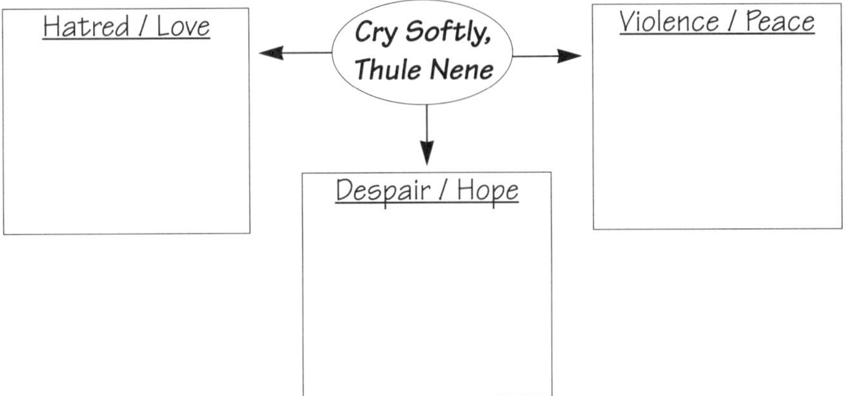

Character judgements

As they read, encourage the pupils to talk about which characters they like and which they dislike. Afterwards, discuss whether and why their opinions of certain characters changed.

Reading skills

Character boxes

Pupils draw boxes in their notebook for each of the main characters. As they read the novel, they fill in words which describe the various characters. These boxes will be used later for paragraph writing (see page 79).

There is an example on the next page.

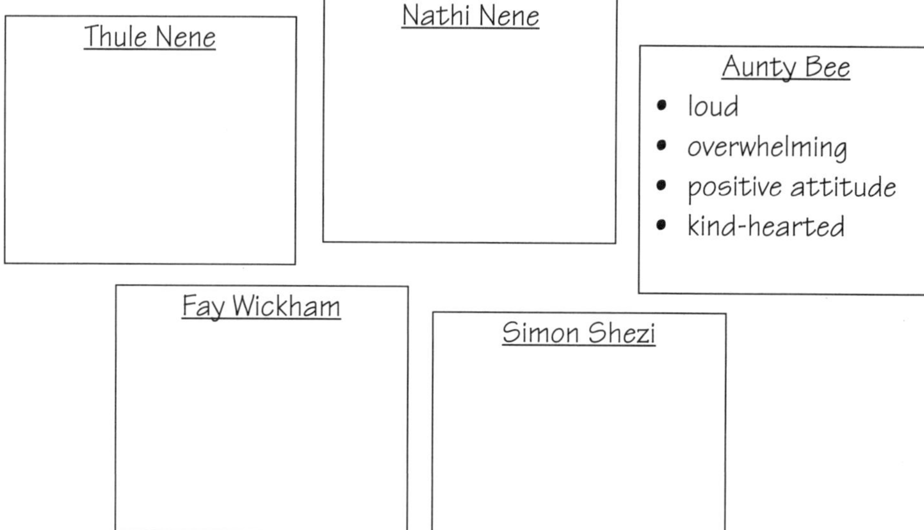

Inferential reading

Allow the pupils to make sense of the novel as a whole. Encourage them to think about events and to make judgements about characters. Stimulate them to infer things from the novel by asking them questions beginning with:

- **How would you ...**
- **What do you think about ...**

Pupils at this level can also start to be critical of books. Encourage critical reviews of the book by asking questions like:

- **Did you enjoy this story? Why?/ Why not?**
- **Do you think the ending is realistic? Give reasons for your answer.**

Language skills

Emotive language

Here are two reactions to a knock on the head:

- 'I have hurt my head rather badly.'

- 'Ouch! Oh! My head hurts! It hurts so much I'm going to cry!'

The first reaction is unemotive, a simple statement of fact. The second uses emotive language to express the feeling vividly, subjectively.

Ask the pupils to identify scenes in the novel where emotive language is used. They should identify the words which make the scene emotive.

Indirect speech

There are many examples of direct speech in the novel (and we discussed this topic earlier, on page 39). Ask the pupils to identify three passages which are written as direct speech. To practise working with indirect or reported speech, get the pupils to tell each other (report) what was being said. They can then rewrite the extracts in indirect speech.

You could also discuss why the author has used direct speech in places. Is it more effective? If so, how?

Plurals

Pupils choose a chapter of the story and scan for plural forms of words. Using the words they have found, they write down some rules for forming plurals of words.

Try out the rule on words which are not given in the plural form in the book. For example: kiss, plait, university.

Writing skills

Paragraph writing

We referred to paragraph writing on page 25. The pupils can build on this by referring to the information that they have recorded in their character boxes (page 78). They can use this information at the end of the novel. Ask the pupils to select a character they like and write a paragraph about that person.

Letter of condolence

Writing, like reading, always has a specific purpose and is usually written for an audience.

> 12 Thrush Street
> Alexandra
> Johannesburg
>
> 15 February 1997
>
> Dear Rachel
>
> I was shocked to hear about the death of your sister in a car accident.
>
> Dudu was a wonderfully warm person who spent her life helping others. The work which she did with the street children in Soweto will always be remembered.
>
> I find it hard to understand how such a young, good person can die. But, sometimes things happen which we cannot understand. It is always more difficult when you lose someone close to you.
>
> Please pass my condolences on to your parents. I will be attending the funeral on Wednesday.
>
> Your friend
>
> Thato

A formal letter is usually structured like this:

- The address of the writer is written on the right-hand side in a block. The date is underneath.

- The greeting is on the left-hand side.
- The letter itself has an opening paragraph, middle paragraphs and a conclusion.
- The final greeting is at the end of the letter and the writer's own name follows.

Get the pupils to write a letter of condolence to Thule.

Writing a report

We looked at report-writing on page 41. In this exercise, we suggest asking the pupils to write a report as the police officer who investigated the massacres at Mpumuza. Allow them to re-read the first chapter to find the information they need to complete the report form.

CRIME REPORT

Type of crime: ____________________

Time and place of crime: ____________________

____

Brief summary of events: ____________________

____

Investigating Officer: ____________________ Date: ______

Remind pupils that reports are clear, factual (unemotive) and brief.

Writing a script

This builds on the activity suggested on page 11. Take a scene from the story and set it out as a script, for example:

Simon: (Kneeling next to Thule) Have you been hurt?

Thule: (Lying on ground) I think I'm all right. I don't seem to have broken any bones.

Simon: (Concerned) I think you should still see a doctor.

Thule: No! I'm fine. I just got a big fright. (She smiles)

Simon: I don't think you should take any chances. (He helps her up)

Point out the elements of script writing shown here:
- direct speech, but no quotation marks
- instructions to actors in brackets.

Ask the pupils what other information would need to be included in a script. They might consider things like descriptions of characters, clothing requirements, details about setting, etc.

Explain to the pupils that this form of writing is to guide actors in films or plays. Let the pupils choose scenes from the story and write them in script form. Allow them to act out their scripts.

Integration

Cry Softly, Thule Nene

Art

Collect advertising posters for films, if these are easily available. Perhaps they could be cut from newspapers or magazines. Let pupils discuss:
- the design and structure of the poster
- the purpose of the poster

Look at the mock-up poster for a film of *Cry Softly, Thule Nene*. Ask your pupils if they think it works effectively; perhaps they could produce their own versions – or create posters for films they have seen.

History

Do a research project on war and violence in Africa. Get pupils to do their own research. Information can be presented as a written report.

Information can come from textbooks and library books. It can also come from the radio or TV news and newspapers.

Life skills

Everyone has to learn to cope with the death of someone close to them at some stage. This is a central theme in the book, and it can be used to prepare pupils for such an event.

Allow pupils to discuss in groups how people react to the death of a loved one. Allow them to talk about their own experiences if this is not too painful for them. Discuss:

- **What assistance can be given to people who have lost a loved one?**
- **How do we talk to such people, and what can we do to make them feel better?**

8 Record-keeping and assessment

Assessing and keeping records of your pupils' reading progress allows you to monitor:

- which skills the pupils have attempted
- which skills need more practice
- which skills have been mastered
- the pupils' level of interest in reading
- the level at which pupils can cope with reading

Here are some of the ideas which we use in our classrooms.

A reading record book

Each pupil has a reading record book (or file), where all written activities are kept together. This makes it easy for you to take material in for marking and assessment.

A reading progress table

JAWS level	Titles read						
1	Wierd Wambo	The Frightened Thief					
Date completed	5/2	20/2					
2			Mr Kalogo's Factory	The Picture That Came Alive			
Date completed			23/3	4/4			
3					The Haunted Taxi Driver		
Date completed							
4							
Date completed							
5							
Date completed							

Pupils draw up and complete a table for themselves like the one started here.

You can tell at a glance which books the pupil has read and also judge their reading level and rate. For easy reference, this table can be pasted on to the inside cover of the reading record book.

Check your own answers

Make answer cards for the questions and written activities at the end of each JAWS book. These answer cards can be stored in a box (a shoebox works well) and used by the pupils to check their own, or each other's, work.

Class record of responses

On a piece of paper, draw up a chart like the one below. You could pin it on a wall, or otherwise make it easily accessible to the pupils. When they have finished reading that particular book, they place a tick on the chart to indicate their response to the book.

Class __________

Title: **Mr Kalogo's Factory (Level 2)**

Too difficult	✓✓✓
Difficult	✓✓✓✓
Just right	✓✓✓✓✓✓✓✓✓✓
Easy	✓✓✓✓✓✓✓✓✓✓

When all the pupils have placed their ticks on the chart, you can consider the overall response to the book. Such a chart allows you to judge whether the book is appropriate for your class level or not.

Keeping detailed records of progress

To monitor pupils' individual progress, you could keep a checklist of skills (based on the grid on pages 6–7). For example:

Pupil's name: Amma Beyala Class: 5(c)		✓ Done * Mastered • Poor, needs help	
Oral skills		**Language skills**	
Discussion	✓	Nouns	✓
Drama	*	Adjectives	
Introductions		Punctuation	•
Sharing opinions		Verbs	✓
Reading skills		**Writing skills**	
Sequencing	•	Poetry	✓
Predicting outcomes		Advertisements	*
The main idea	✓	Paragraphs	•
Summaries		Forms	

If you look at this example, you can see quite quickly that this pupil has done well with activities related to drama and advertisements, but that she needs help in punctuation and paragraphing.

These charts and tables are just some of the ideas that have proved helpful to us. Please feel free to adapt them to meet your own needs in the classroom. As we have emphasised throughout this handbook, our aim is to provide ideas and suggestions to help you make the most of the teaching opportunities afforded by the JAWS readers. Once more, let us wish you all the success and enjoyment that we ourselves have experienced.

Theme chart for JAWS readers

vel 1	Heroines	Relationships	Mystery	Humour	Detective/Thriller	Environment	Adventure
e Big Fight		•					•
ne Bright Lights	•	•					•
aught in the Act	•	•					•
ne Frightened Thief		•					•
ne Girl Who Wouldn't Wear Glasses	•	•		•			
ng Spider		•					
zungu	•	•	•	•			•
othing Ever Happens Here		•					•
abakulu and the Egg Monster	•	•	•			•	•
ne Paper Chase		•					•
xi to Johannesburg		•					•
nandi Goes To Town	•	•		•			
ckles		•				•	•
olley Trouble		•					•
vins in Trouble		•	•				•
/eird Wambo	•	•					•
/inner's Magic		•					•

Level 3	Heroines	Relationships	Mystery	Humour	Detective/Thriller	Environment	Adventure
The African Teapot	•	•	•			•	•
The Artist and the Bully		•					•
The Dancing Suitcase	•	•	•				
The Death Factory	•	•	•			•	
Hamadi and the Stolen Cattle		•			•		•
The Haunted Taxi Driver			•	•	•		•
Kodua's Ark		•		•	•		•
Lindiwi Finds a Way	•	•					•
The Missing Calabash	•	•	•				
Miss John	•	•		•			•
The Old Man and the Rabbit		•					
The Old Warrior		•			•		•
Regina's Dream	•	•		•			
Tikrit		•	•		•		•
The Valley of the Skulls			•		•		•
The Young Builder							
The Young Detectives		•	•		•		•

vel 2	Heroines	Relationships	Mystery	Humour	Detective/Thriller	Environment	Adventure
he Angel Who Wore Shoes		•		•	•		
ne Boy Who Rode a Lion		•		•			•
ne Buried Treasure	•	•	•				•
ottletop Michael		•	•	•	•		•
og Dip	•	•				•	•
ouble Trouble	•	•			•		•
he Empty Water Tank		•		•		•	
he Ghost of Ratemo			•		•		•
appy the Street Child	•	•					
agiso's Mad Uncle		•					•
lasquerade Time		•	•		•		
he Magic Pool	•		•				•
he Midnight Caller			•		•		•
lr Kalogo's Factory		•			•	•	
lr Podee's Poda Poda		•		•			•
he Picture That Came Alive	•		•				
he Prize	•	•					•
he Secret of Nkwe Hill		•	•		•	•	•
he Smile Thief	•		•				
he Strange Piece of Paper	•	•			•		•

Level 4	Heroines	Relationships	Mystery	Humour	Detective/Thriller	Environment	Adventure
Dead Men Don't Talk			•		•		•
Follow the Crow		•	•				•
The Innocent Prisoner		•			•		•
King for Ever!					•		•
The Lonely Stranger		•	•		•		•
Love is a Challenge	•	•	•				•
The Mystery of Mister E		•	•		•	•	•
Paulo's Strange Adventure		•			•	•	•
The Secret Valley		•	•	•			
Street Gang Kid		•	•				•

Level 5	Heroines	Relationships	Mystery	Humour	Detective/Thriller	Environment	Adventure
Cry Softly, Thule Nene	•	•					
The Cruel War		•					•
The Gold Diggers		•	•		•		•
The Ivory Poachers	•	•			•	•	•
Ma'ami	•	•	•		•		•
The Money Game		•		•	•		•
Taxi		•			•		•
The Travellers	•	•	•				•

Ordering JAWS titles

The Junior African Writers Series – JAWS – referred to in this book are a popular series of entertaining and original stories set in Africa. All the stories are written by Africans or authors who have lived in Africa for some time, and so far the series includes stories set in Botswana, Ghana, Kenya, Malawi, Nigeria, Sierra Leone, South Africa and Tanzania. All the books available as of November 1997 are listed in the themes chart on page 87.

Heinemann produces a full catalogue annually giving a complete listing of all titles, which includes an updated themes chart, plus a short description of each title and the country in which the title is set.

If you would like to obtain a catalogue or further information on ordering please contact your closest bookshop or your agent. If you have difficulties, or do not know who your agent is, please contact:

Heinemann
Halley Court
Jordan Hill
Oxford OX2 8EJ
UK

Telephone + 44 (0) 1865 314412
Fax + 44 (0) 1865 314029
Telex 837292 HEBOXF
e-mail export.repp@repp.co.uk